HOOKED THROWS

HOOKED THROWS

20 Easy Crochet Projects

MARGARET HUBERT

**Creative Publishing
international**

CHANHASSEN, MN

Dedication

For my wonderful family

Acknowledgments

I would like to thank Blue Heron Yarns, Caron International, Lion Brand Yarn Company, N.Y. Yarns, Patons Yarns, Plymouth Yarn Company, Tahki/Stacy Charles, Inc., and Trendsetter Yarns, who have graciously donated yarn for most of the projects in this book. Thanks to Paula Alexander, Jeannine Buehler, and Dee Stanziano, who helped me crochet some of the samples, and to my editor, Linda Neubauer, for her help, guidance, and friendship.

Creative Publishing international

Copyright 2006
Creative Publishing international
18705 Lake Drive East
Chanhassen, Minnesota 55317
1-800-328-3895
www.creativepub.com
All rights reserved

President/CEO: Ken Fund
Executive Editor: Alison Brown Cerier
Executive Managing Editor: Barbara Harold
Senior Editor: Linda Neubauer
Photo Stylist: Joanne Wawra
Creative Director: Brad Springer
Photo Art Director: Tim Himsel
Photographers: Steve Galvin and Joel Schnell
Production Manager: Linda Halls
Cover and Book Design: Dania Davey
Cover Layout: Lois Stanfield
Page Layout: Brian Donahue

Printed in China
10 9 8 7 6 5 4 3 2 1

Library of Congress Cataloging-in-Publication Data

Hubert, Margaret.
  Hooked throws : 20 easy crochet projects / Margaret Hubert.
    p. cm.
  ISBN-13: 978-1-58923-267-9 (soft cover)
    ISBN-10: 1-58923-267-4 (soft cover)
  1. Crocheting--Patterns. 2. Throws (Coverlets) I. Title.
  TT825.H7986 2006
  746.43'4041--dc22   2006006266

Visit the following web sites for more information about the yarns shown in this book:

Bernat
www.bernat.com

Berroco, Inc.
www.berroco.com

Blue Heron Yarns
www.blueheronyarns.com

Caron International
www.caron.com

Lion Brand Yarn Company
www.lionbrand.com

N.Y. Yarns
www.nyyarns.com

Patons Yarns
www.patonsyarns.com

Plymouth Yarn Company
www.plymouthyarn.com

Tahki/Stacy Charles, Inc.
www.tahkistacycharles.com

Trendsetter
www.trendsetteryarns.com

Contents

About the Projects

Crochet is easy, fun, fast, and just as popular for home décor items as for fashion. Now you can crochet throws, blankets, and shoulder wraps that will add warmth, softness, and style to your home. Create cuddly baby blankets, colorful mini-blankets for children and teens, or gorgeous throws for your family room or bedroom.

The throws are made in a variety of ways. Some are worked as one big piece, while others are crocheted in strips or blocks and then sewn together. Many of the projects are finished off with an interesting border. Others have fringe or tassels.

For each project, I chose a yarn to complement the stitch and the design of the throw. Cotton yarns and lightweight microfiber yarns are just right for cool evenings of the warmer months. Wool and alpaca yarns offer more warmth for colder months. Smooth yarns show off the texture of crochet and are good for decorative stitches like shells, bobbles, basket weaves, or lace—and they make even single crochet look fascinating. Some throws are made with bulky-weight yarns and crocheted with large hooks, and they work up really fast. Very textured novelty yarns give other throws special character—some are furry and lighthearted, others glitzy and dramatic. With textured yarns, the stitches don't show, so I use simple stitches to let the yarn take center stage.

The projects will be easy for the average crocheter. Some are especially easy and are good beginner projects—after all, there's no fitting involved! Some projects are a bit more challenging, but they offer good chances to learn new stitches. If you need to learn or review a stitch, just go to the basics section at the back of the book for detailed, photographed instructions.

For each project, the materials list will tell you the weight and type of each yarn, as well as the brands, colors, and quantities I used to create the throw in the photograph. You can substitute different yarns of the same weight, and you can certainly choose your own colors. Crochet a sample with your yarn and the hook size suggested to make sure your gauge matches the gauge listed. Luckily, throws and wraps don't have to fit, so small differences in gauge won't matter. The finished size of each project is given. If you want to make your throw or blanket larger, you can add more strips, blocks, or pattern repeats; purchase extra yarn in proportion to the increased size.

If you are new to crochet, I hope this book will help you learn the stitches and inspire you to hook throws for yourself and others. If you have been crocheting for a while, it is my hope that you will enjoy my ideas and patterns and add your own design ideas. Whether this is your first hooked throw or your tenth, enjoy watching your project take shape and become a thing of beauty that will give warmth and comfort to you and those you love.

Margaret Hubert is also the author of Hooked Bags, Hooked Throws, Hooked Scarves, How to Free-Form Crochet, *and six other books. She designs crochet projects for yarn companies and magazines and teaches at yarn shops, retreats, and national gatherings.*

Baby-Soft Blanket

Some yarns today are made with fibers so

soft, you just can't stop touching them. Imagine what a pleasure

it is to crochet with them, feeling baby-soft texture running

through your fingers. This blanket is sure to comfort any baby.

BLANKET
Blanket is worked in 1 piece.

Foundation row: Using A, ch 63 loosely. Beg in third ch from hook, work [1 sc, 1 dc] in same ch, * sk 1 ch, [1 sc, 1 dc] in next ch, rep from * across, end 1 dc in last ch, turn.

Row 1: Ch 2, sk first st and first dc, work [1 sc, 1 dc] in next sc, * sk next dc, [1 sc, 1 dc] in next sc, rep from * across, end 1 dc in top of tch, turn.

Rep row 1, working 10 rows in A, 2 rows in B. (It is okay to carry A loosely up 2 rows of B, but you will have to cut B and restart each time.) Cont in this manner until you have 6 A stripes and 5 B stripes, do not fasten off, turn.

BORDER
Row 1: With right side facing you, cont with A, * work 1 sc in each sc across to corner (62 sts), 3 sc in corner, cont along side, 10 sc in each A section, 2 sc in each B section (70 sc), 3 sc in corner, rep from * once, ending with 3 sc in last corner, join with Sl st to first sc.

Row 2: With A, ch 2, * work 1 hdc in each st to center of next corner, 3 hdc in center of corner, rep from * 3 times more, ending with Sl st to top of beg ch 2, pick up lp with B, fasten off A.

Row 3: With B, rep row 2.

Row 4: With B, * work 1 sc in next st, ch 3, rep from * all around, fasten off.

FINISHING
Weave in ends using tapestry needle.

YARN
Bulky-weight acrylic bouclé and nylon eyelash blend yarn in 2 colors

Shown: Bliss by Caron, 60% acrylic, 40% nylon, 1.75 oz (50 g)/82 yd (75 m): Sky Blue #0010 (A), 7 skeins; Snow #0001 (B), 3 skeins

HOOK
11/L (8 mm)

STITCHES USED
Single crochet
Double crochet
Half double crochet

GAUGE
4½ clusters = 4" (10 cm)
(cluster = 1 sc, 1 dc in same st)

NOTION
Tapestry needle

FINISHED SIZE
36" × 40" (91.5 × 102 cm)

Colorful Weekend Throw

Combine a fun yarn, a large hook, and easy stitches, and you have a throw you can make in a weekend. The yarn constantly changes color as you crochet, which makes it fun to keep going and see what color comes next.

Alternating single and double crochet stitches with super bulky yarn.

THROW

Throw is worked in 1 piece.

Foundation row: Using A, ch 54. Sk 2 ch, * work 1 sc in next ch, 1 dc in next ch, rep from * across, end 1 sc in last ch (52 sts), turn.

Row 1: Ch 3 (counts as a dc), sk first st, * work 1 sc in next dc, 1 dc in next sc, rep from * across, end 1 sc in top of tch, turn.

Rep row 1 until piece measures 36" (91.5 cm) from beg, fasten off.

BORDER

Row 1: With RS facing you, beg in top right corner and, using B, work 1 sc in corner, 1 sc in each st along top to next corner, [1 sc, ch 1, 1 sc] in corner st, cont along row ends, picking up 1 st every other row, down to next corner, [1 sc, ch 1, 1 sc] in corner st, cont in each st along bottom edge to next corner, [1 sc, ch 1, 1 sc] in corner st, cont along side edge, picking up 1 st every other row, back to beg. Work 1 sc in first corner st, ch 1, join with Sl st to first sc.

Row 2: Still using B, work a second row of sc all around, working [1 sc, ch 1, 1 sc] in each corner sp, fasten off B.

Row 3: Using A and foll patt as established, work 1 row all around, fasten off.

FINISHING

Weave in ends using tapestry needle.

YARN

Super bulky weight variegated acrylic/wool blend yarn (A)

Shown: Actions by N.Y. Yarns, 70% acrylic, 30% wool, 1.75 oz (50 g)/49 yd (45 m): color #03, 12 balls

Super bulky weight solid-color wool yarn (B)

Shown: Baby by Tahki/Stacy Charles, 100% merino wool, 3.5 oz (100 g)/60 yd (55 m): color #62, 2 balls

HOOK

11/L (8 mm)

STITCHES USED

Single crochet
Double crochet

GAUGE

6½ sc = 4" (10 cm)

NOTION

Tapestry needle

FINISHED SIZE

36" × 39" (91.5 × 99 cm)

Spicy Stripes Throw

This throw will spice up any room. It is made

with three yarns of similar warm colors but totally

different textures. Crocheted in stripes, they blend

together to make a fascinating throw.

YARN

Bulky-weight acrylic/wool blend yarn (A)

Shown: Wool-Ease Chunky by Lion Brand, 80% acrylic, 20% wool, 5 oz (140 g)/153 yd (140 m): Pumpkin #133, 2 skeins

Bulky-weight acrylic yarn (B)

Shown: Homespun by Lion Brand, 98% acrylic, 2% polyester, 6 oz (170 g)/185 yd (170 m): Coral Gables #370, 2 skeins

Bulky-weight polyester yarn (C)

Shown: Suede by Lion Brand, 100% polyester, 3 oz (85 g)/ 122 yd (110 m): Spice #133, 2 skeins

HOOK

P/Q (15 mm)

STITCHES USED

Single crochet

Double crochet

Reverse single crochet

GAUGE

6 sc = 4" (10 cm)

NOTION

Tapestry needle

FINISHED SIZE

40" × 46" (102 × 117 cm)

Alternating single and double crochet stitches in three-yarn stripe sequence.

THROW

Throw is worked in 1 piece.
Color sequence: 2 rows A, 2 rows B, 2 rows C.

Foundation row: With A, ch 62. Work 1 sc in third ch from hook, * 1 dc in next ch, 1 sc in next ch, rep from * across row (61 sts, counting the st formed by starting in third ch), turn.

Row 1: Ch 3 (counts as a dc), sk first sc, work 1 sc in next dc, *1 dc in next sc, 1 sc in next dc, rep from * across, end last sc in the top of tch, turn.

Foll color sequence, rep row 1 until throw is 44" (112 cm) from beg, ending with 2 rows of A, fasten off.

BORDER

Row 1: With RS facing you, beg in top right corner, using B, ch 1 (half corner), * work 1 sc in each of the next 60 sts, [1 sc, ch 1, 1 sc] in corner, 82 sc evenly spaced along row ends, [1 sc, ch 1, 1 sc] in corner, rep from * once, ending last rep with 1 sc in same st as ch 1, ch 1, join with Sl st to beg ch 1, do not turn.

Three rows of single crochet border finished off with one row of reverse single crochet.

Row 2: Ch 1 (half corner), * work 1 sc in each of next 62 sts, [1 sc, ch 1, 1 sc] in corner sp, 1 sc in each of next 84 sts, [1 sc, ch 1, 1 sc] in corner sp, rep from * once, ending last rep with 1 sc in corner sp, ch 1, join with Sl st to beg ch 1, do not turn.

Row 3: Ch 1 (half corner), * work 1 sc in each of next 64 sts, [1 sc, ch 1, 1 sc] in corner sp, 1 sc in each of next 86 sts, [1 sc, ch 1, 1 sc] in corner sp, rep from * once, ending last rep with 1 sc in corner sp, ch 1, join with Sl st to beg ch 1, do not turn.

Row 4: Work 1 rev sc in each st all around, fasten off.

FINISHING
Weave in ends using tapestry needle.

Alpaca Basket-Weave Throw

The basket-weave effect of this stitch pattern creates a deep, sophisticated texture. It may look complicated, but it is actually easy to make with front post and back post double crochet stitches. This pumpkin-colored yarn is wonderfully soft.

YARN

Bulky-weight bouclé yarn

Shown: Alpaca Bouclé by Plymouth, 90% alpaca, 10% nylon, 1.75 oz (50 g)/70 yd (64 m): color #2037, 20 balls

HOOKS

11/L (8 mm)
10½/K (6.5 mm)

STITCHES USED

Single crochet
Double crochet
Front post double crochet
Back post double crochet
Block stitch

GAUGE

8 dc = 4" (10 cm) on 11/L (8 mm) hook

NOTION

Tapestry needle

FINISHED SIZE

40" × 46" (102 × 117 cm)

Alternating groups of back post and front post double crochet stitches form basket-weave effect.

THROW

Throw is worked in 1 piece.

Foundation row: Using 11/L (8 mm) hook, ch 80. Beg in fourth ch from hook, work 1 dc in each ch (78 dc, counting st formed by starting in fourth ch), turn.

Rows 1, 3, 6, 8: Ch 3 (counts as a dc), sk first st, * FPdc around post of each of next 4 sts, BPdc around post of each of next 4 sts, rep from * across, end FPdc around post of each of next 4 sts, 1 dc in top of tch, turn.

Rows 2, 4, 5, 7: Ch 3 (counts as a dc), sk first st, * BPdc around post of each of next 4 sts, FPdc around post of each of next 4 sts, rep from * across, end BPdc around post of each of next 4 sts, 1 dc in top of tch, turn.

Rep rows 1 through 8 until throw measures 42" (107 cm) from beg, do not fasten off.

BORDER

See page 92 for directions on block st.

Row 1: With RS facing you, beg in top right corner, using 10½/K (6.5 mm) hook, pick up and work 108 sc along side to first corner, [1 sc,

Geometric border of block stitches and double crochet stitches.

ch 2, 1 sc] in corner, 76 sc along bottom to next corner, [1 sc, ch 2, 1 sc] in second corner, 108 sc along other side, [1 sc, ch 2, 1 sc] in third corner, 76 sc along top edge, ending with [1 sc, ch 2, 1 sc] to form fourth corner, join with Sl st to first sc.

Row 2: Ch 3, [work 1 dc in each of next 2 sts, block st, * 1 dc in each of next 3 sts, block st, rep from *] to first corner (27 block sts, 2 dc bet each block), 5 dc in corner ch-2 sp, rep bet [ ] to next corner (19 block sts, 2 dc bet each block), 5 dc in corner ch-2 sp, rep patt for rem 2 sides, join with Sl st to beg ch 3.

Rows 3 and 4: Ch 1, * work 1 sc in each st, 3 sc in center corner st, rep from * around, join with Sl st to beg ch 1, fasten off.

FINISHING
Weave in ends using tapestry needle.

Heirloom Baby Blanket

Dainty shell stitches are traditional for baby

blankets. Using this easy pattern, you can crochet a special

blanket that will become a family keepsake. The blanket is

made in one piece, with rows of shells divided by ridges

formed of front post and back post double crochet stitches.

Front post and back post double crochet stitches form ridges between shells.

YARN

Medium-weight acrylic yarn

Shown: Berella "4" by Bernat, 100% acrylic, 3.5 oz (100 g)/195 yd (178 m): Lilac, 7 skeins

HOOK

8/H (5 mm)

STITCHES USED

Double crochet

Front post double crochet

Back post double crochet

GAUGE

3 shell patterns = 4" (10 cm)

NOTION

Tapestry needle

FINISHED SIZE

30" × 40" (76 × 102 cm)

BLANKET

Blanket is worked in 1 piece.

Foundation row: Ch 121. Starting in fifth ch from hook, * work [2 dc, ch 2, 2 dc] in same st (shell made), sk 2 ch, 1 dc in next ch, sk 2 ch, rep from * across, end sk 2 ch, 1 dc in last ch (20 shells), turn.

Row 1: Ch 3, * work [2 dc, ch 2, 2 dc] in next ch-2 sp, 1 FPdc over next dc, rep from * across, end 1 dc in top of tch, turn.

Row 2: Ch 3, * work [2 dc, ch 2, 2 dc] in next ch-2 sp, 1 BPdc over next dc, rep from * across, end 1 dc in top of tch, turn.

Rep rows 1 and 2 for 40" (102 cm), fasten off.

FINISHING

Weave in ends using tapestry needle.

Big Waves Throw

Ride the wave! When you crochet a basic pattern

using chunky yarn and a large hook, you can finish

in record time. This exciting throw has bold colors

and contemporary style.

YARN

Super bulky weight solid-color wool yarn in 3 colors

Shown: Baby by Tahki/Stacy Charles, 100% merino wool, 3.5 oz (100 g)/60 yd (55 m): color #63 (green) (A), 5 skeins; color #60 (rose) (B), 6 skeins; color #49 (blue) (C), 4 skeins

HOOK
P/Q (15 mm)

STITCHES USED
Single crochet

Half double crochet

Double crochet

Triple crochet

Reverse single crochet

GAUGE
6 sc = 4" (10 cm)

NOTION
Tapestry needle

FINISHED SIZE
34" × 40" (86.5 × 102 cm)

23

Waves rise and fall as stitches progress from single to half double to double to triple crochet and back again.

THROW

Throw is worked in 1 piece.

Color sequence: * [2 rows A, 2 rows B, 2 rows A], 2 rows C, rep from * 5 times more, rep bet [ ] once.

Row 1 (RS): With A, ch 47. Work 1 sc in second ch from hook, 1 sc in each ch to end of row (46 sc), turn.

Row 2: With A, ch 1 (counts as first sc), sk first st, work 1 sc in each sc, turn.

Row 3: With B, ch 3 (counts as first dc), sk first sc, work 1 dc in next sc, 1 hdc in next sc, 1 sc in next sc, * ch 2, sk 2 sc, 1 sc in next sc, 1 hdc in next sc, 1 dc in each of next 2 sc, 1 tr in each of next 2 sc, 1 dc in each of next 2 sc, 1 hdc in next sc, 1 sc in next sc, rep from * 2 more times to last 6 sts, ch 2, sk 2 sc, 1 sc in next sc, 1 hdc in next sc, 1 dc in next sc, 1 dc in top of tch, turn.

Row 4: With B, ch 3 (counts as first dc) sk first dc, work 1 dc in next dc, 1 hdc in next hdc, 1 sc in next sc, * ch 2, sk 2 sts , 1 sc in next sc, 1 hdc in next hdc, 1 dc in each of next 2 dc, 1 tr in each of next 2 tr, 1 dc in each of next 2 dc, 1 hdc in next hdc, 1 sc in next sc, rep from * 2 more times to last 6 sts, ch 2, sk 2 sts , 1 sc in next sc, 1 hdc in next hdc, 1 dc in next dc, 1 dc in top of tch, turn.

Row 5: With A, ch 1 (counts as first sc), sk first st, work 1 sc in each of next 3 sts, [inserting hook from front of work, work 1 sc in each of 2 free sc in A 3 rows below], * 1 sc in each of next 10 sts, rep bet [ ], rep from * to last 4 sts, 1 sc in each of next 3 sts, 1 sc in top of tch, turn.

Row 6: With A, ch 1 (counts as first sc), sk first st, work 1 sc in each sc, 1 sc in top of tch, turn.

Border of double crochet stitches is finished off with a row of reverse single crochet.

Row 7: With C, ch 1 (do not sk first st on this row), * work 1 sc in next sc, 1 hdc in next sc, 1 dc in each of next 2 sc, 1 tr in each of next 2 sc, 1 dc in each of next 2 sc, 1 hdc in next sc, 1 sc in next sc, ch 2, sk 2 sc, rep from * across, omitting ch 2 at end of last rep, end 1 sc in top of tch, turn.

Row 8: With C, ch 1 (does not count as first sc), * work 1 sc in next sc, 1 hdc in next hdc, 1 dc in each of next 2 dc, 1 tr in each of next 2 tr, 1 dc in each of next 2 dc, 1 hdc in next hdc, 1 sc in next sc, ch 2, sk 2 sts, 1 sc next sc, rep from * 3 times more, omitting ch 2 at end of last rep, end 1 sc in top of tch, turn.

Row 9: With A, ch 1 (counts as first sc), sk first st, * work 1 sc in each of next 10 sts, inserting hook from front of work, work 1 sc in each of 2 free sc in A 3 rows below, 1 sc in each of next 10 sts, rep from * 2 more times, end last rep with 1 sc in each of last 9 sts, 1 sc in top of tch, turn.

Foll color sequence, rep rows 2 through 9 five times more, then rep rows 2 through 6, fasten off.

BORDER
Row 1: With right side facing you, join B in top right corner, ch 3 (half corner), * work 1 dc in each st to next corner (48 dc), 3 dc in corner st, pick up 54 dc evenly spaced down side to next corner, 3 dc in corner st, rep from * once more, end 2 dc in same st as beg ch, join with Sl st to top of beg ch 3, do not turn.

Row 2: Work 1 row rev sc all around, fasten off.

FINISHING
Weave in ends using tapestry needle.

Glitzy Wrap

Multi-fiber yarns are spun together from fibers of a variety of textures and colors. The yarn in this shoulder wrap blends warm mohair with shiny fibers for some glamour. Pull it around your shoulders in the evening while you're watching a movie! The pattern is worked from a center foundation row in both directions, so the lacy shells all face outward and create scallops at both narrow ends.

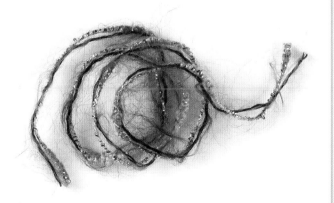

YARN
Bulky-weight multi-fiber yarn

Shown: Dune by Trendsetter, 41% mohair, 30% acrylic, 12% viscose, 11% nylon, 6% metal, 1.75 oz (50 g)/90 yd (82 m): color #58, 9 balls

HOOK
10¹/₂/K (6.5 mm)

STITCHES USED
Single crochet
Double crochet
Triple crochet

GAUGE
1 shell cluster = 2³/₄" (7 cm)

NOTION
Tapestry needle

FINISHED SIZE
20" × 68" (51 × 173 cm)

27

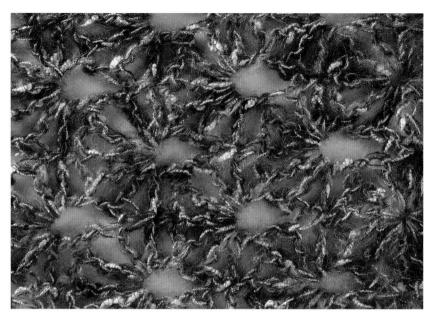

Lacy open-work pattern of triple crochet shells.

FIRST HALF OF WRAP

Wrap is worked in 2 halves, both starting from same center ch.

Foundation row: Ch 57. Sc in second ch from hook, sk 3 ch, * work [tr, ch 2] 4 times in next ch, 1 more tr in same ch (shell CL made), sk 3 ch, sc in next ch, rep from * 6 times more (7 shell CL), turn.

Row 1: Ch 5 (counts as 1 tr, ch 2), work 1 dc in the first ch-2 sp, * ch 3, sk next ch-2 sp, 1 sc in top of third tr of shell CL, ch 3, sk next ch-2 sp, 1 dc in next ch-2 sp, ch 2, 1 dc in next ch-2 sp, rep from * 5 times more, end ch 3, 1 sc in third tr of shell CL, ch 3, sk next ch-2 sp, 1 dc in next ch-2 sp, ch 2, 1 tr in last sc, turn.

Row 2: Ch 5 (counts as 1 tr, ch 2), work [1 tr, ch 2, 1 tr] in first tr (half shell CL made), * 1 sc in next sc, [1 tr, ch 2] 4 times in next ch-2 sp, 1 more tr in same sp, rep from * 5 times more, end 1 sc in next sc, [1 tr, ch 2, 1 tr, ch 2, 1 tr] all in third ch of tch (half shell CL made) (half shell CL at beg of row, 6 full shell CL, half shell CL at end of row), turn.

Each end of wrap is scalloped because wrap is worked from center out in both directions.

Row 3: Ch 1, work 1 sc in first tr, ch 3, 1 dc in second ch-2 sp, * ch 2, 1 dc in next ch-2 sp, ch 3, 1 sc in third tr of CL, ch 3, sk 1 ch-2 sp, 1 dc in next ch-2 sp, rep from * 5 times more, end 1 dc in next ch-2 sp, ch 3, 1 sc in third ch of tch, turn.

Row 4: Ch 1, work 1 sc in first sc, * [tr, ch 2] 4 times in next ch-2 sp, 1 more tr in same sp, 1 sc in next sc, rep from * 6 times more (7 shell CL), turn.

Rep rows 1 through 4 for 34" (86.5 cm), ending with row 4, fasten off.

SECOND HALF OF WRAP
Join yarn in right corner of beg ch. Working on other side of ch, rep patt beg at foundation row, fasten off.

FINISHING
Weave in ends using tapestry needle.

Delicate Web Wrap

Spider web—the small, alternating shell pattern in

this shoulder wrap—looks like vintage lace. Made of

lightweight microfiber yarn, the wrap is not only

ultrasoft and feminine, but also warm.

YARN

Lightweight microfiber yarn

Shown: Microspun by Lion Brand, 100% microfiber acrylic, 2.5 oz (70 g)/168 yd (154 m): Mocha #124, 8 skeins

HOOK

8/H (5 mm)

STITCHES USED

Single crochet

Double crochet

GAUGE

4 shell clusters = 4" (10 cm)

NOTION

Tapestry needle

FINISHED SIZE

25" × 60" (63.5 × 152.5 cm)

Staggered placement of shell clusters results in a delicate, lacy web of stitches.

WRAP

Wrap is worked in 1 piece.

To create the staggered placement of shells from row to row, odd rows beg and end with a half CL, even rows beg and end with a full CL.

Foundation row: Ch 110. Starting in second ch from hook, work 1 sc, * sk 2 ch, [1 dc, ch 1, 1 dc, ch 1, 1 dc] in next ch (shell CL made), sk 2 ch, 1 sc in next ch, rep from * across, end 1 sc in last ch (18 shell CL).

Row 1: Ch 4 (counts as 1 dc, ch 1), work 1 dc in first sc, sk 1 dc, 1 sc in next dc (center of shell), sk next dc, *[1 dc, ch 1, 1 dc, ch 1, 1 dc] in next sc, sk 1 dc, 1 sc in next sc, sk next dc, rep from * across, end [1 dc, ch 1, 1 dc] in last st (17 full shell CL and a half shell on each end), turn.

Row 2: Ch 1, work 1 sc in first dc, * [1 dc, ch 1, 1 dc, ch 1, 1 dc] in next sc, sk 1 dc, 1 sc in next dc, rep from * across, end sk 1 dc, [1 dc, ch 1, 1 dc, ch 1, 1 dc] in next sc, 1 sc in next dc, 1 sc in third ch of tch (18 full shell CL), turn.

Rep rows 1 and 2 until wrap is 58" (147 cm) long, do not fasten off.

Scalloped shell border perfectly finishes the edges of the wrap.

BORDER

With right side facing you, ch 3, work 2 dc in same st (this is half of the first corner). Working along long edge of wrap, * work [3 dc, ch 2, 3 dc] in next sp (created by turning chains), 1 sc in next sp, rep from * to bottom, [3 dc, ch 2, 3 dc] in last st (second corner), rep from * working along foundation ch to last st, work corner in last st, cont up other long edge, work corner in last st, cont along top edge, ending with 3 dc in same st as beg, join with Sl st to form last corner, fasten off.

FINISHING

Weave in ends using tapestry needle.

Double-Up Wrap

This shoulder wrap is made by crocheting together two yarns of totally different textures using an extra-large hook. One yarn has mohair and other fibers that make the wrap warm and fuzzy. The other yarn is a smooth, shiny ladder yarn. This wrap can be finished fast, and the result is stunning.

Ladder yarn and multi-fiber yarn held together and worked in single crochet with a large hook.

YARN

Bulky-weight multi-fiber yarn

Shown: Moonlight Mohair by Lion Brand, 35% mohair, 30% acrylic, 25% cotton, 10% polyester metallic, 1.75 oz (50 g)/82 yd (75 m): Safari #203, 5 balls

HOOK

P/Q (15 mm)

STITCH USED

Single crochet

GAUGE

6 sc = 4" (10 cm)

NOTIONS

Tapestry needle

8" (20.5 cm) piece of cardboard

FINISHED SIZE

15" × 52" (38 × 132 cm) not including fringe

WRAP

Wrap is worked in 1 piece, with 1 strand of each yarn held tog throughout.

Foundation row: Ch 23 loosely. Starting in second ch from hook, work 1 sc in each ch across (22 sc), turn.

Row 1: Ch 1 (counts as a sc), sk first st, work 1 sc in each st across, 1 sc in tch, turn.

Rep row 1 until piece measures 52" (132 cm), fasten off.

FINISHING

Weave in ends using tapestry needle.

FRINGE

Wrap both yarns around 8" (20.5 cm) piece of cardboard 44 times. Cut yarn at bottom to make 44 double strands, each 16" (40.5 cm) long. Fold a double strand in half and, using a crochet hook, pull lp through first st at one narrow end of wrap. Put tails of double strand through lp and pull tails to snug lp up to edge of wrap. Rep at each st across both ends of wrap.

Sherbet Triangle Wrap

To create this unusual shoulder wrap, you start at the point and work toward the top. The yarn is dyed in a rainbow of colors that change as you hook along. The crosshatch stitch pattern is fun to work as you watch the colors develop into a complex and very beautiful surface.

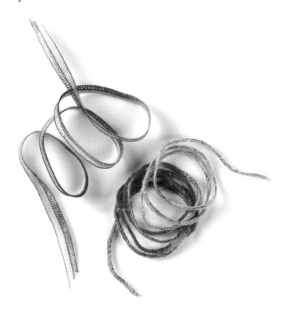

YARN

Lightweight smooth yarn for throw

Shown: Rayon/Metallic by Blue Heron, 85% rayon, 15% metallic, 8 oz (227 g)/550 yd (506 m): Sunrise, 1 skein

Medium-weight ribbon yarn for fringe

Shown: Zen by Berroco, 55% cotton, 45% nylon, 1.75 oz (50 g)/110 yd (102 m): Skakti Mix #8181, 2 balls

HOOK

9/I (5.5 mm)

STITCH USED

Double crochet

GAUGE

5 clusters = 4" (10 cm)
(1 cluster = ch 3, 3 dc in same ch lp)

NOTIONS

Tapestry needle
9" (23 cm) piece of cardboard

FINISHED SIZE

52" × 24" (132 × 61 cm), not including fringe

Lightweight rayon/metallic yarn worked in double crochet clusters.

WRAP

Wrap is worked in 1 piece from lower point to long upper edge.

Row 1: Ch 5 (counts as a dc, called ch lp now and throughout), work 3 dc into fifth ch from hook (1 CL made, 4 sts total), turn.

Row 2: Ch 5, work 3 dc into fifth ch from hook, Sl st into ch lp of next CL, ch 3, work 3 dc into same ch lp (2 CL made), turn.

Row 3: Ch 5, work 3 dc into fifth ch from hook, Sl st into ch lp of next CL, ch 3, work 3 dc into same ch lp, Sl st into ch lp of next CL, ch 3, work 3 dc into same ch lp (3 CL made), turn.

Row 4: Ch 5, work 3 dc into fifth ch from hook, Sl st into ch lp of next CL, ch 3, work 3 dc into same ch lp, Sl st into ch lp of next CL, ch 3, work 3 dc into same ch lp, Sl st into ch lp of next CL, ch 3, work 3 dc into same ch lp (4 CL made).

Cont to work in this manner, beg every row with ch 5, 3 dc into fifth ch from hook, CL in each ch lp across row, ending with CL in last ch lp. You will have 1 more CL at the end of each row. Work until the entire ball of yarn is used (about 50 rows).

Last row of clusters at upper edge forms dainty scallops.

FINISHING
Weave in ends using tapestry needle.

FRINGE
Wrap ribbon yarn around 9" (23 cm) piece of cardboard about 300 times. Cut yarn at bottom to make 300 strands, each 18" (46 cm) long. Fold 2 strands in half and, using a crochet hook, pull lp through st at lower point of wrap. Put tails of double strand through lp, and pull tails to snug lp up to edge of wrap. Rep along both diagonal sides of wrap, evenly spacing about 75 fringes on each side.

Tunisian Stripes Throw

Hooked in vibrantly colored cotton yarn, Tunisian

crochet makes a dense fabric perfect for a

summer-weight throw. Step-by-step directions for

Tunisian crochet are on page 92.

YARN

Medium-weight cotton yarn in 3 colors

Shown: Cotton Classic II by Tahki/Stacy Charles, 100% cotton, 1.75 oz (50 g)/74 yd (68 m): Green #2726 (A), 6 skeins; Periwinkle #2882 (B), 7 skeins; Turquoise #2815 (C), 6 skeins

HOOK

10½/K (6.5 mm) Tunisian hook

STITCHES USED

Tunisian (basic)
Single crochet
Double crochet

GAUGE

13 sc = 4" (10 cm) in Tunisian crochet

NOTION

Tapestry needle

FINISHED SIZE

42" × 44" (107 × 112 cm)

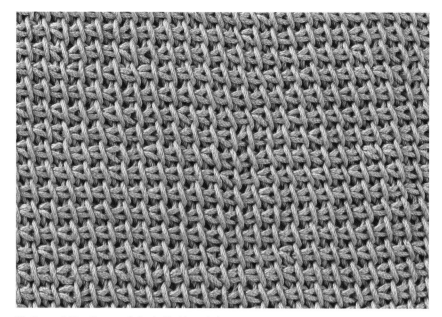

Medium-weight cotton yarn in basic Tunisian stitch.

THROW

Throw is made in 5 strips that are sewn tog.

In basic Tunisian st, each row refers to both a forward and a return pass. Forward pass is picking up all lps on hook. Return pass is working them off. You are always working from RS. See page 92 for complete instructions for Tunisian st.

STRIPS 1 AND 5

Foundation row: With A, ch 20. Pick up lp in second ch from hook and retain on hook. Retaining all lps on hook, pick up lp in each st across ch, do not turn. Yo, draw through first lp on hook, * yo, draw through 2 lps on hook, rep from * to end of row, do not turn.

Row 1: Pick up lp under each vertical bar on prev row. Retaining all lps on hook, yo, draw through first lp on hook, * yo, draw through 2 lps on hook, rep from * to end of row.

Rep row 1 for 107 rows more, do not fasten off.

Outer edge: Ch 3 (half corner), * work 1 dc in each st across to next corner (20 dc), [1 dc, ch 2, 1 dc] in corner st, cont to work dc in row ends, picking up 108 sts, work [1 dc, ch 2, 1 dc] in next corner st, rep from *

Double-crochet shell-stitch border frames the throw.

once, ending last rep with 1 dc in same st as beg ch 3, ch 2, join with Sl st to top of ch 3 (completes last corner), fasten off.

STRIPS 2 AND 4
With B, work same as strips 1 and 5.

STRIP 3
With C, ch 40, work Tunisian st same as strips 1 and 5. Work outer edge same as strips 1 and 5, but work 40 dc across short ends.

FINISHING
Sew strips tog using tapestry needle and foll photo for color sequence. Weave in ends.

BORDER
With RS facing you, join B in top right corner, ch 3, work 2 dc in corner sp (half corner), [* sk 2 sts, sc in next st, sk 2 sts, (3 dc, ch 2, 3 dc) in next st (shell made), rep from * 19 times more, **sk 2 sts, shell in corner sp, sk 2 sts, sc in next st, sk 2 sts, shell in next st, rep from ** 17 times more, sk 2 sts, shell in corner st], rep bet [ ] once, ending with 3 dc in same corner sp as beg, ch 2, join with Sl st to beg ch 3.

Bumpy Road Blanket

Bobble stitches and cross stitches give this throw the intricate look of an Aran sweater. The bobbles are crocheted from the wrong side and popped through to the front. There are directions with photos for both stitches on page 91. Made in strips, the blanket is surprisingly easy to crochet and works up quickly.

YARN

Medium-weight smooth yarn

Shown: Encore Worsted Weight by Plymouth, 75% acrylic, 25% wool, 3.5 oz (100 g)/200 yd (184 m): color #2764, 9 skeins

HOOK

8/H (5 mm)

STITCHES USED

Single crochet

Double crochet

Bobble stitch

Cross stitch

GAUGE

11 dc = 4" (10 cm)

NOTION

Tapestry needle

FINISHED SIZE

38" × 40" (96.5 × 102 cm)

BLANKET

Blanket is worked in 5 strips and then sewn tog.

STRIPS 1 AND 5: Foundation row (RS): Ch 26. Beg, in fourth ch from hook, work 1 dc in each ch (23 dc), turn.

Row 1 (WS): Ch 1 (counts as a sc), sk first st, work 1 sc in each of next 2 sts, 1 bobble st in next st (push bobble to RS), * 1 sc in each of next 3 sts, 1 bobble st in next st, rep from * 3 times more, end 2 sc, 1 sc in top of tch (5 bobble sts in all), turn.

Rows 2–4: Ch 3 (counts as a dc), sk first st, work 1 dc in each st across, 1 dc in top of tch (23 dc), turn.

Row 5: Ch 1 (counts as a sc), sk first st, work 1 sc in each of next 4 sts, 1 bobble st in next st, * 1 sc in each of next 3 sts, 1 bobble st in next st, rep from * 2 times more, end 1 sc in each of next 4 sts, 1 sc in top of tch (4 bobble sts in all), turn.

Rows 6–8: Rep rows 2–4.

Rep rows 1–8 eight more times, then rep rows 1 and 2 once (75 rows in all, counting foundation row), fasten off.

STRIPS 2 AND 4: Foundation row (RS): Ch 21. Beg in fourth ch from hook, work 1 dc in each ch (18 dc), turn.

Row 1 (WS): Ch 1 (counts as a sc), sk first st, work 1 sc in each st, 1 sc in top of tch (18 sc), turn.

Row 2: Ch 3 (counts as a dc), sk first st, work 1 dc in each st, 1 dc top of tch (18 dc), turn.

Row 3: Ch 3 (counts as a dc), sk first st and next dc, work 1 dc in next dc, 1 dc in second skipped st, * sk 1 st, 1 dc in next st, 1 dc in skipped st, rep from * 6 times more, end 1 dc in top of tch (8 cross sts, 1 dc each side), turn.

Row 4: Rep row 2.

Rep rows 1–4 17 times more, then rep rows 1 and 2 once (75 rows in all, counting foundation row), fasten off.

STRIP 3: Foundation row (RS): Ch 26. Beg in fourth ch from hook, work 1 dc in each ch (23 dc), turn.

Row 1 (WS): Ch 1 (counts as a sc), sk first st, work 1 sc in each st, 1 sc in top of tch (23 sc), turn.

Rows 2–4: Ch 3 (counts as a dc), sk first st across, work 1 dc in each st, 1 dc in top of tch (23 dc), turn.

Row 5: Rep row 1.

Rows 6–8: Rep rows 2–4.

Row 9 (beg diamond patt): Ch 1 (counts as a sc), sk first st, work 1 sc in each of next 10 sts, 1 bobble st in next st, 1 sc in each of next 10 sts, 1 sc in top of tch (11 sc each side, 1 bobble st in center), turn.

Rows 10–12: Ch 3 (counts as a dc), sk first st, work 1 dc in each st across, 1 dc in top of tch (23 dc), turn.

Row 13: Ch 1 (counts as a sc), sk first st, work 1 sc in each of next 5 sts, 1 bobble st in next st, 1 sc in each of next 9 sts, 1 bobble st in next st, 1 sc in each of next 5 sts, 1 sc in top of tch (2 bobble sts, 21 sc), turn.

Rows 14–16: Rep rows 10–12.

Row 17: Ch 1 (counts as a sc), sk first st, work 1 sc in each of next 2 sts, 1 bobble st in next st, 1 sc in each of next 7 sts, 1 bobble st in next st, 1 sc in each of next 7 sts, 1 bobble st in next st, 1 sc in each of next 2 sts, 1 sc in top of tch (3 bobble sts, 20 sc), turn.

Rows 18–20: Rep rows 10–12.

Row 21: Rep row 13.

Rows 22–24: Rep rows 10–12.

Row 25: Rep row 9.

Rows 26–28: Rep rows 10–12.

Rows 29–68: Rep rows 9–28 two times.

Rows 69–72: Rep rows 1–4.

Rows 73 and 74: Rep rows 1 and 2 (75 rows in all, counting foundation row), fasten off.

FINISHING
Sew strips 1 through 5 tog, left to right, using tapestry needle. Weave in ends.

BORDER
Row 1: With RS facing you, join yarn in top right corner, ch 1, * work sc in each st to next corner (106 sc), [1 sc, ch 1, 1 sc] in corner st, cont along side edge, picking up 2 sc in each sp created by dc at end of rows (112 sc), [1 sc, ch 1, 1 sc] in corner st, rep from * once, ending last rep with 1 sc in last st, ch 1, join with Sl st to beg ch 1, do not turn.

Row 2: Ch 3 (half corner), * [sk next st, work 1 dc in next st, 1 dc in skipped st], rep bet [ ] to next corner, (1 dc, ch 2, 1 dc) in corner sp, cont along side edge, rep bet [ ] to next corner, (1 dc, ch 2, 1 dc) in corner sp, rep from * once, ending last rep with 1 dc in last st, ch 2, join with Sl st to top of beg ch 3 (completes beg corner).

Row 3: Ch 1, work 1 sc in each st around, making 3 sc in each corner sp, fasten off.

Sunflower Throw

Add some sunshine to your bedroom, den, or porch.

This throw is made in strips of alternating solid and

mesh squares that go together like a checkerboard.

Accenting all the solid squares are cheerful sunflowers

that are fun to crochet.

YARN
Medium-weight acrylic yarn for throw

Shown: Canadiana by Patons, 100% acrylic, 3.5 oz (100 g)/201 yd (185 m): Light Juniper #00050, 7 skeins

Lightweight cotton yarn in 2 colors for sunflowers

Shown: Cotton Classic by Tahki/Stacy Charles, 100% cotton, 1.75 oz (50 g)/108 yd (100 m): #3537 (yellow), 1 skein; #3317 (brown), 1 skein

HOOKS
10/J (6 mm)
6/G (4 mm)

STITCHES USED
Single crochet
Half double crochet
Double crochet
Triple crochet

GAUGE
10 dc = 4" (10 cm) on 10/J (6 mm) hook

NOTIONS
Tapestry needle
Stitch marker

FINISHED SIZE
40" × 49" (102 × 125 cm)

THROW

Throw is made in 5 strips and then sewn tog.

Strips 1, 3, and 5 beg and end with solid dc patt, alternated with mesh patt.

Strips 2 and 4 beg and end with mesh patt, alternated with solid dc patt.

STRIPS 1, 3, AND 5

Foundation row: Using medium-weight acrylic yarn and 10/J (6 mm) hook, ch 21. Beg in fourth ch, work 1 dc in each ch (19 dc, counting st formed by starting in fourth ch from hook), turn.

Row 1: Ch 3 (counts as a dc), sk the first st, work 1 dc in each of next 17 dc, 1 dc in top of tch (19 dc), turn.

Rows 2–10: Rep row 1.

Row 11: Ch 5 (counts as 1 dc, ch 2), sk first 2 sts, work 1 dc in next dc, * ch 2, sk 1, 1 dc in next dc, rep from * 7 times more, end 1 dc in third ch of tch (9 sps, 10 dc), turn.

Rows 12–20: Rep row 11.

Row 21: Ch 3, work 1 dc in first sp, 2 dc in each sp across, end 1 dc in third ch of tch (19 dc), turn.

Rows 22–30: Rep row 21.

Rows 31–50: Rep rows 11–30, fasten off.

STRIPS 2 AND 4

Foundation row: Ch 21. Beg in fifth ch from hook (counts as 1 dc, ch 2), work 1 dc, * ch 2, sk 1 ch, 1 dc in next ch, rep from * 7 times more (9 sps, 10 dc), turn.

Rows 2–10: Rep row 11 of strips 1, 3, and 5.

Rows 11–20: Rep rows 21–30 of strips 1, 3, and 5.

Rows 21–30: Rep rows 11–20 of strips 1, 3, and 5.

Rows 31–50: Rep rows 21–40 of strips 1, 3, and 5.

SUNFLOWERS
Make 18.

With lightweight brown cotton yarn and 6/G (4 mm) hook, beg at flower center, ch 4, join with Sl st to form ring.

Rnd 1: Work 8 sc in ring, pm, do not join.

Rnd 2: Work 2 sc in each sc around (16 sc), bring up marker, do not join.

Rnd 4: * Work 1 sc in first sc, 2 sc in next sc, rep from * around (24 sc), bring up marker, do not join.

Rnd 5: Rep rnd 4 (36 sc), join with Sl st to first sc, fasten off brown.

Join yellow from WS in any outer rnd st on flower center, * ch 5, turn. Working along ch and starting in second ch from hook, work 1 sc, 1 dc, 2 tr, sk 2 sc on flower center, Sl st in next st (1 petal made). Rep from * 11 times more (12 petals in all), fasten off.

FINISHING
Weave in ends using tapestry needle. Sew sunflowers to centers of solid squares in each strip. Sew strips tog.

BORDER
Row 1: With RS facing you, beg in top right corner, join yarn, ch 1 (half corner), * work in sc along edge to next corner, picking up 102 sts, [1 sc, ch 3, 1 sc] in corner st, cont in sc along side to next corner, picking up 112 sts, [1 sc, ch 3, 1 sc] in corner st, rep from * once, ending with 1 sc in last st, ch 3, join with Sl st to beg ch 1.

Row 2: Ch 3 (counts as a dc), sk first st, * work 1 dc in each st to corner, [1 dc, ch 3, 1 dc] in corner sp, rep from * all around, ending with Sl st to top of beg ch 3.

Row 3: Ch 1 (counts as a sc), sk first st, [*work 1 hdc, 1 dc, 1 tr, 1 dc, 1 hdc, 1 sc, rep from * to corner (17 scallops), (1 hdc, 1 dc, 1 tr, 1 dc, 1 hdc, 1 sc) in corner ch-3 sp, sk 1 st, rep from * to next corner (19 scallops), (1 hdc, 1 dc, 1 tr, 1 dc, 1 hdc, 1 sc) in corner sp], rep bet [ ] once, join with Sl st to beg ch 1.

Row 4: * [Ch 3, work 1 sc in next st] 5 times, sk 2 sts, 1 sc in next st, rep from * all around, end with Sl st at base of beg ch 3, fasten off.

Fur Checks Throw

This crazy, cuddly throw is a checkerboard of fur yarn and smooth yarn. Made in stripes, it's quick and easy to crochet. The tassels are a fun finishing touch.

YARN

Medium-weight smooth yarn (A)

Shown: Wool-Ease by Lion Brand, 80% acrylic, 20% wool, 3 oz (85 g)/197 yd (180 m): Turquoise #148, 5 skeins

Bulky-weight novelty fur yarn (B)

Shown: Fun Fur by Lion Brand, 100% polyester, 1.75 oz (50 g)/ 60 yd (54 m): Turquoise #148, 6 skeins

HOOKS

10½/K (6.5 mm)

11/L (8 mm)

STITCHES USED

Single crochet

Half double crochet

Three-chain bobble

GAUGE

10½ sc = 4" (10 cm) on both hooks

NOTIONS

Tapestry needle

8" (20.5 cm) piece of cardboard

FINISHED SIZE

34" × 46" (86.5 × 117 cm)

Three-chain bobbles give the smooth-yarn squares a pebbly look.

THROW

Throw is made in 5 strips and then sewn tog.

To attain the same gauge for the medium-weight smooth yarn and the fur, it is necessary to change hooks when you change yarns while working the strips.

STRIPS 1, 3, AND 5

Foundation row: Beg with A (smooth yarn) and 10½/K (6.5 mm) hook, ch 18. Work 1 sc in each ch (17 sc), turn.

Row 1: Ch 1, Sl st in first st (do not sk 1), pick up lp in next st, and in that lp ch 3, yo, and pull through both lps on hook, * work 1 sc in next st, pick up lp in next st, and in that lp ch 3, yo, and pull through both lps, rep from * 6 times more, end 1 sc in last st (8 bobbles), turn.

Row 2: Ch 1 (counts as sc), sk first st, work 1 sc in each of next 15 sts, 1 sc in tch, turn.

Rep rows 1 and 2 for 6½" (16.3 cm). Pull up last lp with B (fur yarn). Change to 11/L (8 mm) hook and work B in sc for 6½" (16.3 cm).

Cont to work 6½" (16.3 cm) of bobble patt with A and smaller hook and 6½" (16.3 cm) of sc with B and larger hook until 7 blocks have been completed, fasten off.

Hefty tassels dangle from the corners.

STRIPS 2 AND 4

With yarn B and larger hook, ch 18. Work as strips 1, 3, and 5 alternating 6½" (16.3 cm) B in sc and 6½" (16.3 cm) of A until 7 blocks have been completed, fasten off.

FINISHING

Sew strips tog using tapestry needle, matching blocks to form the checkerboard patt. Weave in ends.

BORDER

Row 1: With A and smaller hook, join yarn in top right corner, RS facing you, ch 3 in corner (half corner). * Work in sc, picking up 16 sc in each block (80 sc along top), [1 hdc, ch 2, 1 hdc] in corner sp (full corner), cont down side, working 16 sc in each block (112 sc), [1 hdc, ch 2, 1 hdc] for next corner, rep from * once, ending with 1 hdc in last st, ch 2, join with Sl st to top of beg ch 3 to complete last corner.

Row 2: * Work 1 sc in next st, 1 bobble in next st, rep from * to next corner, [1 hdc, ch 2, 1 hdc] in corner ch-2 sp, rep from * all around, join with Sl st to beg sc.

Row 3: * Work 1 sc in each st to next corner, [1 sc, ch 2, 1 sc] in corner ch-2 sp, rep from * all around, ending with Sl st to beg sc, fasten off.

TASSELS

Make 4.

Cut eight 18" (46 cm) pieces of yarn A and set aside for ties. Using 8" (20.5 cm) piece of cardboard, wrap yarn A around cardboard 30 times. Tie top of tassel tightly using long piece of yarn, leaving long tails to attach tassel to corner of throw. Slide tassel from cardboard and cut bottom lps. Using another long piece, tie tassel about 1½" (3.8 cm) from top. Let the tie ends become part of tassel. Tie 1 tassel to each corner. Thread tails of ties down into tassels. Trim ends.

Baby Diamonds Blanket

This entrelac baby blanket is worked in adjoining strips of squares turned on their points. The pattern is a little challenging at first, but once mastered, it is quite easy. The blanket is worked in Tunisian crochet, but you can use a regular hook because there are never more than seven stitches on the hook at a time.

YARN

Medium-weight acrylic yarn in 3 colors

Shown: Canadiana by Patons, 100% acrylic, 3.5 oz (100 g)/201 yd (185 m): aqua #045 (MC), 4 balls; white #001 (A), 2 balls; light yellow #169 (B), 2 balls

HOOK

9/I (5.5 mm)

STITCHES USED

Tunisian

Single crochet

Double crochet

GAUGE

1 square = 1½" (3.8 cm)

NOTION

Tapestry needle

FINISHED SIZE

34" × 42" (86.5 × 107 cm)

Interlocking squares of Tunisian crochet are turned on their points.

BLANKET

Entrelac patt is worked entirely from RS. When 1 strip is completed, fasten off that yarn, join new yarn at beg of row, and start again. To even out ends, every other color strip begins and ends with a half square (triangle). Each square or triangle in strip consists of 5 rows. Refer to page 92 for detailed instructions for Tunisian st.

STRIP 1
Begins and ends with triangle.

With MC, ch 144 loosely.

Beg Triangle, Row 1: Draw up lp in second ch from hook (2 lps on hook), yo, draw through both lps.

Row 2: Insert hook bet first 2 vertical bars and pick up lp (inc made), pick up lp in next ch (3 lps on hook), [yo, draw through 2 lps] 2 times (1 lp left on hook).

*Row 3: Insert hook bet first 2 bars and pick up lp (inc made), draw up lp from under next bar and next ch (4 lps on hook), [yo, draw through 2 lps] 3 times (1 lp left on hook).

Cont in this manner, having 1 st more each row, until you have 7 lps on hook (row 5), work off as before.

Bind off: Insert hook under next bar, draw yarn through bar and lp on hook (Sl st worked). Cont to work Sl st through each bar to end.* Sl st in same ch as last lp of row 5. Do not fasten off, but cont to first square.

Square 1, Row 1 (still on first color strip): Draw up lp in each of next 6 ch (7 lps on hook), [yo, draw through 2 lps] 6 times (1 lp left on hook). This lp is the first lp of the foll row.

Row 2: Insert hook under next bar, draw yarn through (2 lps on hook), draw up lp in each of next 4 bars, draw up lp in next ch (7 lps on hook), work off lps as for row 1 of square.

Rows 3–5: Rep row 2.

Bind off: Sl st in each bar to end, Sl st in same ch as last lp of row 5.

Squares 2–13: Work same as square 1 (6 ch left at end of row).

End Triangle, Row 1 (end of first color strip): Draw up lp in each of 6 rem ch (7 lps on hook), work off as before.

Row 2: Draw up 5 lps (6 lps on hook), work off as before.

Cont in this manner, always having 1 less lp each row, until 1 lp rem, fasten off. This completes first color strip.

STRIP 2
Begins and ends with a square. Each square has 5 rows.

Square 1, Row 1: With A, pick up 1 lp in each of 6 Sl sts of beg triangle, pick up lp in end of first row of first square on strip 1 (7 lps on hook), work off lps.

Complete square as for rows 2–5 of square 1 of first strip.

Bind off: Sl st in each bar to end, having last Sl st in last row (top point) of same square.

Squares 2–14: Work same as square 1, picking up first row of sts in slipped sts, then under bars in subsequent rows. End strip with completed square.

Peaks of the border echo the blanket's diamond motif.

STRIP 3
Begins and ends with a triangle.

Beg Triangle: With MC, ch 2, draw up lp in first ch from hook and pick up lp in side of first row of first square of strip 2 (3 lps on hook), [yo, draw through 2 lps] 2 times. Rep from * to * of beg triangle, strip 1. Sl st in first bound off st of square 1, strip 2.

Work squares of strip same as squares of strip 2. End with triangle, same as end triangle, strip 1.

REMAINING STRIPS
Work same as strips 2 and 3 in this color sequence: B, MC, A, MC, ending with MC (39 strips).

CLOSING TRIANGLES
Worked across top and bottom to even off edges.

Row 1: With MC, at top right corner, pick up 6 lps along bound off edge of first square, plus 1 lp in end of first row of second square (7 lps on hook), work off as before.

Row 2: Sk first bar, pick up 5 lps so you only have 6 lps on hook, work off as before.

Row 3: Sk first bar, pick up 4 lps (5 lps on hook), work off as before.

Row 4: Sk first bar, pick up 3 lps (4 lps on hook), work off as before.

Row 5: Sk first bar, pick up 2 lps (3 lps on hook), work off as before, 1 lp on hook, Sl st into last side st (at top).

Cont across top edge in this manner. Work same closing triangles across bottom edge.

BORDER
Row 1: Using MC, starting in top right corner, RS facing you, ch 1, work 1 sc in same st (half corner), * work sc along short edge, picking up 96 sts along this end, 3 sc in corner, sc along long end, picking up 126 sts along this end, 3 sc in corner, rep from * once, ending with 1 sc in same st as beg, join with Sl st to beg ch 1 (this forms last corner).

Row 2: Ch 3, work 2 dc in same st (half corner), * sk 2 sts, 1 sc in next st, sk 2 sts, [3 dc, ch 2, 3 dc] in next st, rep from * all around, ending with 3 dc in same st as beg ch 3, ch 2, join with Sl st to form last corner, fasten off.

FINISHING
Weave in ends using tapestry needle.

Rainbow Blocks Blanket

This colorful blanket is a great gift for a toddler or preschooler.

Because it will get lots of use, the blanket is crocheted from

yarn that can be machine laundered. The rainbow blocks are

actually crocheted in strips that can be sewn together quickly.

Machine washable yarn in tiny shell pattern of single crochet and chain stitches.

BLANKET

Color sequence of squares in each strip (left to right):
Strip 1: red, green, rose, yellow, orange, blue, red
Strip 2: green, rose, yellow, orange, blue, red, blue
Strip 3: rose, yellow, orange, blue, red, blue, orange
Strip 4: yellow, orange, blue, red, blue, orange, yellow
Strip 5: orange, blue, red, blue, orange, yellow, rose
Strip 6: blue, red, blue, orange, yellow, rose, green
Strip 7: red, blue, orange, yellow, rose, green, red

Foll the above color sequence, make 7 strips as foll:

Foundation row: Ch 22. Starting in third ch from hook, *work [1 sc, ch 2, 1 sc] all in same ch (small shell made), sk 1, rep from * across, end 1 hdc in last ch, turn (7 small shells).

Row 1: Ch 2 (counts as a hdc), * work [1 sc, ch 2, 1 sc] all in ch-2 sp of next small shell, rep from * 6 times more, end 1 hdc in top of tch, turn.

Rep row 1 for 5" (12.7 cm). Pull up new color on last row, and cont next color in sequence. Cont in this manner until all 7 color blocks are made. Fasten off.

FINISHING

Sew all strips tog using tapestry needle. Weave in ends.

BORDER

Row 1: With blue, RS facing you, join yarn in any corner. Working in sc, work 1 sc in corner (half corner), * 14 sc in each color block, [1 sc, ch 1, 1 sc] in corner, rep from * 3 times more, ending with 1 sc in last st, ch 1, join with Sl st to first sc (completing corner).

Row 2: Ch 3 (half corner), * [sk 1 sc, work 1 dc in next sc, 1 dc in skipped sc] 49 times, [1 dc, ch 2, 1 dc] in ch-1 sp of corner, rep from * 3 times more, ending with 1 dc in last st, ch 2, join with Sl st in last corner sp.

RAINBOW BLOCKS BLANKET

YARN
Medium-weight smooth yarn in 6 colors

Shown: Encore Worsted Weight by Plymouth, 75% acrylic, 25% wool, 3.5 oz (100 g)/200 yd (184 m): blue #4045, 2 skeins; yellow #1382, 1 skein; orange #1383, 1 skein; rose #1385, 1 skein; red #1386, 1 skein; green #3335, 1 skein

HOOK
10/J (6 mm)

STITCHES USED
Single crochet
Half double crochet
Double crochet

GAUGE
5 small shells = 4" (10 cm)

NOTION
Tapestry needle

FINISHED SIZE
36" × 36" (91.5 × 91.5 cm)

Handsome Plaid Throw

A den or home office is the perfect place for this plaid throw of grays and cream. This would be a great gift for a man. The plaid is easier than it looks. There are five strips with a ridge of front post and back post double crochet stitches down the center of each strip.

YARN

Medium-weight smooth yarn in 3 colors

Shown: Encore Worsted Weight by Plymouth, 75% acrylic, 25% wool, 3.5 oz (100 g)/200 yd (184 m): light gray #194 (A), 5 skeins; charcoal gray #520 (B), 3 skeins; aran #256 (C), 3 skeins

HOOK

10/J (6 mm)

STITCHES USED

Single crochet

Half double crochet

Front post double crochet

Back post double crochet

GAUGE

11 hdc = 4" (10 cm)

NOTION

Tapestry needle

FINISHED SIZE

42" × 56" (107 × 142 cm)

Medium-weight acrylic/wool blend yarn in half double crochet stitches.

THROW

Throw is made in 5 strips and then sewn tog.

Work strips 1, 3, and 5 in color sequence as foll: * [8 rows A, 2 rows C, 8 rows A], 8 rows C, 2 rows B, 8 rows C, rep from * twice more, rep bet [ ] once more, fasten off.

Work strips 2 and 4 in color sequence as foll: * [8 rows A, 2 rows C, 8 rows A], 18 rows B, rep from * twice more, rep bet [ ] once more, fasten off.

Foundation row: Ch 25. Starting in third ch from hook, * work 1 hdc in next ch, rep from * 21 times more (23 hdc, counting st formed by starting in third ch), turn.

Row 1: Ch 2 (counts as a hdc), sk first st, * 1 hdc in next st, rep from * 9 times more (11 hdc), 1 FPdc under bar of next st, 1 hdc in each of next 10 sts, 1 hdc in top of tch (11 hdc on each side of FPdc), turn.

Row 2: Rep row 1, except work a BPdc over center st.

Rep rows 1 and 2, foll color sequence for each strip, fasten off.

Single crochet stitches accent the front post and back post double crochet stitch ridges.

FINISHING

Fold strip 1 in half lengthwise, WS tog, so center posts are on edge. Using color B, beg at bottom, inserting hook under posts of sts, work 2 sc under each post to top, fasten off. Rep for each rem strip, using color B on strips 3 and 5 and color C on strips 2 and 4. Sew strips tog using tapestry needle, matching plaid as shown in photo. Weave in ends.

BORDER

With color B, join yarn in top right corner, RS facing you, ch 2 (half corner), * work 1 hdc in each st across to corner (115 hdc), 3 hdc in corner st, cont down side, working 21 sc in each large color block (147 hdc), 3 hdc in corner st, rep from * once, ending last rep with 2 hdc in same st as beg, join with Sl st to top of ch 2, fasten off.

Quartet Throw

Show off your skills with a sampler throw of four squares in four different stitches. Chunky yarn crocheted with a large hook gives the stitches a bold look. For a larger, rectangular throw, buy more yarn and repeat your two favorite squares.

YARN

Bulky-weight smooth yarn

Shown: Encore Chunky by Plymouth, 75% acrylic, 25% wool, 3.5 oz (100 g)/143 yd (131 m): color #133, 10 balls

HOOK

10½/K (6.5 mm)

STITCHES USED

Single crochet

Double crochet

Tunisian

Front post triple crochet

GAUGE

Square 1 (fan stitch): 1 fan, 3 sc, 1 fan = 5" (12.7 cm)

Square 2 (caterpillars): 5 dc and FPtr = 4" (10 cm)

Square 3 (cluster stitch): 4 clusters = 4" (10 cm)

Square 4 (Tunisian and shells): 2 Tunisian squares = 5" (12.7 cm)

NOTION

Tapestry needle

FINISHED SIZE

40" × 40" (102 × 102 cm)

Square 1 is staggered rows of double crochet stitch fans and V stitches.

THROW

Throw is made in 4 squares and then sewn tog. Make 1 of each square.

SQUARE 1 (FAN STITCH)

Row 1 (RS): Ch 62. Work 1 sc in second ch from hook, 1 sc in next ch, *
sk 3 ch, work fan of [3 dc, ch 1, 3 dc] in next ch, sk 3 ch, 1 sc in next ch,
ch 1, sk 1 ch, 1 sc next ch, rep from * 5 times more, end 1 sc in each of
last 2 ch (6 fans), turn.

Row 2: Ch 4 (counts as 1 dc, ch 1), sk first sc, work 1 dc in next sc, * ch 3,
1 sc in ch-1 sp in center of fan, ch 3, V st of [1 dc, ch 1, 1 dc] in next ch-1
sp (bet 2 sc), rep from * 4 times more, end ch 3, 1 sc in ch-1 sp in fan, ch
3, [1 dc, ch 1, 1 dc] in top of tch, turn.

Row 3: Ch 3, work 3 dc in first st (half fan), * 1 sc in next ch-3 sp, ch 1, 1
sc in next ch-3 sp, work fan in ch-1 sp at center of next V st, rep from * 4
times more, end 1 sc in ch-3 sp, ch 1, 1 sc in next ch-3 sp, 4 dc in top of
tch (half fan), turn.

Row 4: Ch 1, work 1 sc in first st, ch 3, V st in next ch-1 sp, ch 3, 1 sc in
sp in center of next fan, rep from * 4 times more, end ch 3, V st in next ch-
1 sp, ch 3, 1 sc in top of tch, turn.

Row 5: Ch 1, work 1 sc in first st, * 1 sc in next ch-3 sp, fan in ch-1 sp of
next V st, 1 sc in next ch-3 sp, rep from * 5 times more, end 1 sc in tch,
turn.

Caterpillars of square 2 are rows of front post triple crochet stitches.

Rep rows 2 through 5 for 20" (51 cm), ending with row 4, do not fasten off. Ch 1, work 41 sc across row, 3 sc in corner, 41 sc down row ends to next corner, 3 sc in corner, 41 sc along bottom, 3 sc in corner, 41 sc up other side, ending with 3 sc in last st, join with Sl st to beg ch 1, fasten off.

SQUARE 2 (CATERPILLARS)
Foundation row (RS): Ch 48. Sk 3 ch (counts as a dc), work 1 dc into each ch to end of row (45 dc), turn.

Row 1: Ch 1 (counts as a sc), sk first st, work 1 sc in each st to end, working last st in top of tch (45 sc), turn.

Row 2: Ch 3 (counts as a dc), sk first st, * work 1 FPtr around dc below next st, 1 dc in next st, rep from * across, end last dc in top of tch, turn.

Row 3: Rep row 1.

Row 4: Ch 3 (counts as a dc), sk first st, * work 1 dc in next st, 1 FPtr around dc below next st, rep from * to last 2 sts, 1 dc in last st, 1 dc top of tch, turn.

Rep rows 1 through 4 for 20" (51 cm), do not fasten off. Work 1 row sc around entire edge as in square 1, fasten off.

SQUARE 3 (CLUSTER STITCH)
Foundation row (RS): Ch 48. Sk 2 ch (counts as a sc), work 2 dc in next ch, * sk 2 ch, [1 sc, 2 dc] in next ch, rep from * to last 3 ch, sk 2 ch, 1 sc in last ch, turn.

Clusters of one single crochet and two double crochet stitches repeated every row form square 3.

Row 1: Ch 1, (counts as a sc), work 2 dc in first st, * sk 2 dc, [1 sc, 2 dc] in next sc, rep from * to last 3 sts, sk 2 dc, 1 sc in top of tch, turn.

Rep row 1 for 20" (51 cm), do not fasten off. Work 1 row sc around entire piece as in square 1, fasten off.

SQUARE 4 (TUNISIAN AND SHELLS)
Foundation: Ch 60.

Row 1 (shells): Work 4 dc in fourth ch from hook, * sk 3 ch, 1 sc in next ch, sk 3 ch, 9 dc in next ch, rep from * 4 times more, end sk 3 ch, 1 sc next ch, sk 3 ch, 5 dc in last ch, ch 1, turn.

Row 2 (Tunisian st, RS): * [Draw up lp in next st and retain lp on hook] 5 times (6 lps on hook), draw up lp in next st and draw this lp through first lp on hook forming an upright st or bar, [yo and through 2 lps] 5 times. * There are 6 bars in row and 1 lp on hook. ** Lp on hook counts as first st so sk first bar, retaining lps on hook, and draw up lp in each of next 5 bars (6 lps on hook), draw up lp in next st and through first lp on hook, [yo and through 2 lps] 5 times, rep from ** 2 times more. Insert hook in second bar, yo and through bar and lp on hook (1 st bound off), bind off 4 more sts, 1 sc in next st. Rep from * 5 times more, end bind off 5 sts, sc in top of tch, ch 1, turn.

Row 3: Sk first st (ch 1 counts as first st), work 1 sc in second st and in each st to end, 1 sc in top of tch, ch 3, turn.

Row 4 (first part of shell row): Yo, draw up lp in second sc, yo and through 2 lps on hook, [yo and draw up lp in next st, yo and through 2 lps]

Diamonds of Tunisian stitch alternate with shells in square 4.

3 times, yo and through 5 lps on hook, ch 1 tightly for eye of half shell. * Ch 3, work 1 sc in next st, ch 3, [yo and draw up lp in next st, yo and through 2 lps] 9 times, yo and through 10 lps on hook, ch 1 tightly to form eye of full shell, rep from * 4 times more, end ch 3, 1 sc in next st, ch 3, [yo and draw up lp in next st, yo and through 2 lps] 4 times, yo and through 5 lps, ch 1 tightly to form eye of half shell, ch 3, turn.

Row 5 (second part of shell row): Work 4 dc in eye of first half shell, sk ch 3, 1 sc in first sc, sk ch 3, * 9 dc in eye of next shell, sk ch 3, 1 sc in next sc, sk ch 3, rep from * 4 times more, end sk ch 3, 4 dc in eye of last half shell, 1 dc in top of tch, ch 1, turn.

Rep rows 2 through 5 for 20" (51 cm), ending with row 4, do not fasten off. Work 1 row sc around entire piece as in square 1, fasten off.

FINISHING
Sew all 4 squares tog as in photo, using tapestry needle. Weave in ends.

BORDER
With RS facing you, join yarn in any corner st, ch 3, work 2 dc in same st (half corner), [* sk 2 sts, (1 dc, ch 1, 1 dc) in next st, sk 2 sts, (3 dc, ch 1, 3 dc) in next st, rep from *12 times more, sk 2 sts, (1 dc, ch 1, 1 dc) in next st, sk 2 sts, (3 dc, ch 1, 3 dc) in corner st]. Rep bet [ ] 3 times more, ending last rep with 3 dc, in same st as beg half corner, ch 1, join with Sl st to beg ch 3 (completes corner), fasten off.

3-D Granny Squares

Granny squares are always popular. One reason is that you work on only one small piece at a time, so you can take it wherever you go. This new granny-square pattern has a different twist that creates an illusion of depth.

YARN

Medium-weight smooth yarn in 4 colors

Shown: Suri Merino by Plymouth, 55% suri alpaca, 45% super fine merino wool, 1.75 oz (50 g)/110 yd (100 m): tan #208 (MC), 6 balls; blue #5297 (A), 2 balls; orange #2037 (B), 5 balls; beige #282 (C), 4 balls

HOOK

8/H (5 mm)

STITCHES USED

Single crochet

Double crochet

Double triple crochet

GAUGE

Each square = 5" (12.7 cm)

NOTION

Tapestry needle

FINISHED SIZE

30" × 46" (76 × 117 cm)

Double triple crochet stitches form diagonal bars across the granny squares.

THROW

Throw is made in 40 squares and then sewn tog.

Double triple crochet (dtr): Wrap yarn 3 times around hook, pick up lp in designated st, [yo and through 2 lps] 4 times.

Foundation rnd: With A, ch 6, join with Sl st to form ring.

Rnd 1: Ch 3 (counts as dc), work 3 dc, ch 3, * 4 dc, ch 3, rep from * 2 times more, join with Sl st to top of beg ch 3 (4 groups of 4 dc), fasten off A.

Rnd 2: Join MC in any ch-3 sp, ch 3, * work 2 dc in same ch-3 sp, 1 dc in each of next 4 dc, 2 dc in next ch-3 sp, 1 dtr, inserting hook from front to back, going into beg ring and bet groups of dc, rep from * 3 times more, join with Sl st to beg ch 3, draw up lp with B, fasten off MC.

Rnd 3: With B, ch 3 (counts as dc), work 1 dc in first st, 1 dc in each of next 7 dc, 2 dc in next dc, ch 3 (corner), * 2 dc in next dc, 1 dc in each of next 7 dc, 2 dc in next dc, ch 3 (corner), rep from * 2 times more, join with Sl st to top of beg ch 3, fasten off B.

Rnd 4: Join C in any ch-3 sp, ch 3, * work 2 dc same ch-3 sp, 1 dc in each of next 11 dc, 2 dc in next ch-3 sp, 1 dtr, inserting hook from right to left

Single crochet stitches through the back loop form ridges on each side of the double crochet row in the border.

under dtr on rnd 2, rep from * 3 times more, join with Sl st to top of beg ch 3, draw up lp with MC, fasten off C.

Rnd 5: With MC, ch 1, * work 1 sc in each of next 16 sts, ch 2, rep from * 3 times more, end with Sl st to beg ch 1, fasten off.

FINISHING

Using tapestry needle, sew squares tog in 8 rows of 5 squares each, sewing from WS, tbl of last row, leaving ridge on RS of work. Weave in ends.

BORDER

Row 1: With RS facing you, join MC in top right corner and, in ch-2 sp of first square, ch 1, (half corner), * work in sc tbl, working 1 sc in each st to next corner, [1 sc, ch 2, 1 sc] in corner sp, rep from * 3 times more, ending with ch 2, join with Sl st to beg ch 1, do not turn.

Row 2: Ch 3 (half corner), * work 1 dc in each st to next corner, [1 dc, ch 2, 1 dc] in corner sp, rep from * 3 times more, ending with 1 dc in next corner sp, ch 2, join with Sl st to top of beg ch 3, do not turn.

Row 3: Ch 1 (half corner), rep from * in row 1, fasten off.

Turning Corners Blanket

Dimension is created by crocheting mitered squares in increasingly lighter shades of a single color. Each square has dark bands on the left side and bottom, with gradually lighter bands ending in a very light square at the top right.

YARN

Medium-weight acrylic yarn in 4 shades of 1 color

Shown: Canadiana by Patons, 100% acrylic, 3.5 oz (100 g)/201 yd (185 m): Stonewash #114 (A), 4 skeins; Denim #110 (B), 2 skeins; Faded Denim #0118 (C), 2 skeins; Light Blue #128 (D), 1 skein

HOOK

10½/K (6.5 mm)

STITCH USED

Single crochet

GAUGE

12 sc = 4" (10 cm)

NOTION

Tapestry needle

FINISHED SIZE

45" × 55½" (115 × 141 cm)

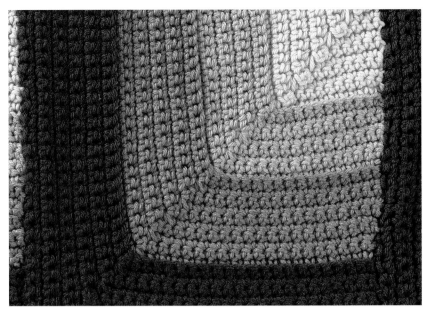

Single crochet 3 stitches together to turn square corners at centers of rows.

BLANKET

Blanket is made in 20 squares and then sewn tog.

Single crochet 3 stitches together (sc3tog): Pick up lp in next 3 sts, yo and pull through all 4 lps on hook.

Foundation row (WS): With A, ch 58. Work 1 sc in second ch from hook, 1 sc in each ch (57 sc), turn.

Row 1: Ch 1 (counts as sc now and throughout), sk first sc, work 1 sc in each of next 26 sc, sc3tog, 1 sc in each of next 26 sc, 1 sc top of tch (55 sc), turn.

Row 2: Ch 1, sk first st, work 1 sc in each st across row, 1 sc in top of tch, turn.

Row 3: Ch 1, sk first st, work 1 sc in each of next 25 sc, sc3tog, 1 sc in each of next 25 sc, 1 sc in top of tch (53 sc), turn.

Row 4: Rep row 2.

Row 5: Ch 1, sk first st, work 1 sc in each of next 24 sc, sc3tog, 1 sc in each of next 24 sc, 1 sc in top of tch (51 sc), turn.

Row 6: Rep row 2.

Row 7: Ch 1, sk first st, work 1 sc in each of next 23 sc, sc3tog, 1 sc in each of next 23 sc, 1 sc in top of tch (49 sc), turn.

Row 8: Rep row 2.

Row 9: Ch 1, sk first st, work 1 sc in each of next 22 sc, sc3tog, 1 sc in each of next 22 sc, 1 sc in top of tch (47 sc), turn.

Row 10: Rep row 2, pull up B through last st, fasten off A.

Row 11: Work this row tbl. Ch 1, sk first st, work 1 sc in each of next 21 sc, sc3tog, 1 sc in each of next 21 sc, 1 sc in top of tch (45 sc), turn.

Row 12: Rep row 2.

Row 13: Ch 1, sk first st, work 1 sc in each of next 20 sc, sc3tog, 1 sc in each of next 20 sc, 1 sc in top of tch (43 sc), turn.

Row 14: Rep row 2.

Row 15: Ch 1, sk first st, work 1 sc in each of next 19 sc, sc3tog, 1 sc in each of next 19 sc, 1 sc in top of tch (41 sc), turn.

Row 16: Rep row 2.

Row 17: Ch 1, sk first st, work 1 sc in each of next 18 sc, sc3tog, 1 sc in each of next 18 sc, 1 sc in top of tch (39 sc), turn.

Row 18: Rep row 2.

Row 19: Ch 1, sk first st, work 1 sc in each of next 17 sc, sc3tog, 1 sc in each of next 17 sc, 1 sc in top of tch (37 sc), turn.

Row 20: Rep row 2, pull up C through last st, fasten off B.

Row 21: Work this row tbl. Ch 1, sk first st, work 1 sc in each of next 16 sc, sc3tog, 1 sc in each of next 16 sc, 1 sc in top of tch (35 sc), turn.

Row 22: Rep row 2.

Row 23: Ch 1, sk first st, work 1 sc in each of next 15 sc, sc3tog, 1 sc in each of next 15 sc, 1 sc in top of tch (33 sc), turn.

Row 24: Rep row 2.

Row 25: Ch 1, sk first st, work 1 sc in each of next 14 sc, sc3tog, 1 sc in each of next 14 sc, 1 sc in top of tch (31 sc), turn.

Row 26: Rep row 2.

Row 27: Ch 1, sk first st, work 1 sc in each of next 13 sc, sc3tog, 1 sc in each of next 13 sc, 1 sc in top of tch (29 sc), turn.

Row 28: Rep row 2, pull up D through last st, fasten off C.

Row 29: Work this row tbl. Ch 1, sk first st, work 1 sc in each of next 12 sc, sc3tog, 1 sc in each of next 12 sc, 1 sc in top of tch, turn (27 sc).

Row 30: Ch 1, sk first st, work 1 sc in each of next 11 sc, sc3tog, 1 sc in each of next 11 sc, 1 sc in top of tch (25 sc), turn.

Row 31: Ch 1, sk first st, work 1 sc in each of next 10 sc, sc3tog, 1 sc in each of next 10 sc, 1 sc in top of tch (23 sc), turn.

Row 32: Ch 1, sk first st, work 1 sc in each of next 9 sc, sc3tog, 1 sc in each of next 9 sc, 1 sc in top of tch (21 sc), turn.

Row 33: Ch 1, sk first st, work 1 sc in each of next 8 sc, sc3tog, 1 sc in each of next 8 sc, 1 sc in top of tch (19 sc), turn.

Row 34: Ch 1, sk first st, work 1 sc in each of next 7 sc, sc3tog, 1 sc in each of next 7 sc, 1 sc in top of tch (17 sc), turn.

Row 35: Ch 1, sk first st, work 1 sc in each of next 6 sc, sc3tog, 1 sc in each of next 6 sc, 1 sc in top of tch (15 sc), turn.

Row 36: Ch 1, sk first st, work 1 sc in each of next 5 sc, sc3tog, 1 sc in each of next 5 sc, 1 sc in top of tch (13 sc), turn.

Row 37: Ch 1, sk first st, work 1 sc in each of next 4 sc, sc3tog, 1 sc in each of next 4 sc, 1 sc in top of tch (11 sc), turn.

Row 38: Ch 1, sk first st, work 1 sc in each of next 3 sc, sc3tog, 1 sc in each of next 3 sc, 1 sc in top of tch (9 sc), turn.

Row 39: Ch 1, sk first st, work 1 sc in each of next 2 sc, sc3tog, 1 sc in each of next 2 sc, 1 sc in top of tch (7 sc), turn.

Row 40: Ch 1, sk first st, work 1 sc in next sc, sc3tog, 1 sc in next sc, 1 sc in top of tch (5 sc), turn.

Row 41: Ch 1, sk first st, sc3tog, 1 sc in top of tch (3 sc), turn.

Row 42: Ch 1, sk 1, pick up next st, yo through both, fasten off.

FINISHING

Using tapestry needle, sew squares tog in 5 rows of 4 squares each, with the darkest sides of each square at left and bottom.

BORDER

When sewn tog, with RS facing you, throw will have dark border on left and bottom. To complete border, join A in bottom right corner. Working in sc, pick up 29 sts in each square to top (145 sc), work 3 sc in corner to turn, cont along top edge, working 29 sts in each square (116 sc), ch 1, turn. Cont in this manner, working in sc, always working 3 sts in the center st of corner, for 9 rows more, fasten off.

Crochet Stitches

SLIP KNOT AND CHAIN

All crochet begins with a chain, into which is worked the foundation row for your piece. To make a chain, start with a slip knot. To make a slip knot, make a loop several inches from the end of the yarn, insert the hook through the loop, and catch the tail with the end **(1).** Draw the yarn through the loop on the hook **(2).** After the slip knot, start your chain. Wrap the yarn over the hook (yarn over) and catch it with the hook. Draw the yarn through the loop on the hook. You have now made 1 chain. Repeat the process to make a row of chains. When counting chains, do not count the slip knot at the beginning or the loop that is on the hook **(3).**

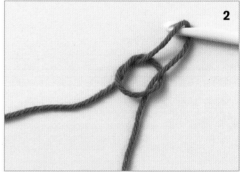

SLIP STITCH

The slip stitch is a very short stitch, which is mainly used to join 2 pieces of crochet together when working in rounds. To make a slip stitch, insert the hook into the specified stitch, wrap the yarn over the hook **(1)** and then draw the yarn through the stitch and the loop already on the hook **(2)**.

SINGLE CROCHET

Insert the hook into the specified stitch, wrap the yarn over the hook, and draw the yarn through the stitch so there are 2 loops on the hook **(1)**. Wrap the yarn over the hook again and draw the yarn through both loops **(2)**. When working in single crochet, always insert the hook through both top loops of the next stitch, unless the directions specify front loop or back loop only.

SINGLE CROCHET 2 STITCHES TOGETHER

This decreases the number of stitches in a row or round by 1. Insert the hook into the specified stitch, wrap the yarn over the hook, and draw the yarn through the stitch so there are 2 loops on the hook **(1)**. Insert the hook through the next stitch, wrap the yarn over the hook, and draw the yarn through the stitch so there are 3 loops on the hook **(2)**. Wrap the yarn over the hook again and draw the yarn through all the loops at once.

 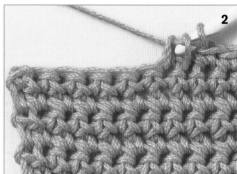

SINGLE CROCHET 3 STITCHES TOGETHER

This decreases the number of stitches in a row or round by 2. Follow the directions for sc2tog, but draw up a loop in the third stitch so there are 4 loops on the hook before wrapping the yarn and drawing through all the loops at once.

SINGLE CROCHET THROUGH THE BACK LOOP

This creates a distinct ridge on the side facing you. Insert the hook through the back loop only of each stitch, rather than under both loops of the stitch. Complete the single crochet as usual.

REVERSE SINGLE CROCHET

This stitch is usually used to create a border. At the end of a row, chain 1 but do not turn. Working backward, insert the hook into the previous stitch **(1)**, wrap the yarn over the hook, and draw the yarn through the stitch so there are 2 loops on the hook. Wrap the yarn over the hook again and draw the yarn through both loops. Continue working in the reverse direction **(2)**.

HALF DOUBLE CROCHET

Wrap the yarn over the hook, insert the hook into the specified stitch, and wrap the yarn over the hook again **(1)**. Draw the yarn through the stitch so there are 3 loops on the hook. Wrap the yarn over the hook and draw it through all 3 loops at once **(2)**.

DOUBLE CROCHET

Wrap the yarn over the hook, insert the hook into the specified stitch, and wrap the yarn over the hook again. Draw the yarn through the stitch so there are 3 loops on the hook **(1)**. Wrap the yarn over the hook again and draw it through 2 of the loops so there are now 2 loops on the hook **(2)**. Wrap the yarn over the hook again and draw it through the last 2 loops **(3)**.

TRIPLE, OR TREBLE, CROCHET

Wrap the yarn over the hook twice, insert the hook into the specified stitch, and wrap the yarn over the hook again. Draw the yarn through the stitch so there are 4 loops on the hook. Wrap the yarn over the hook again **(1)** and draw it through 2 of the loops so there are now 3 loops on the hook **(2)**. Wrap the yarn over the hook again and draw it through 2 of the loops so there are now 2 loops on the hook **(3)**. Wrap the yarn over the hook again and draw it through the last 2 loops **(4)**.

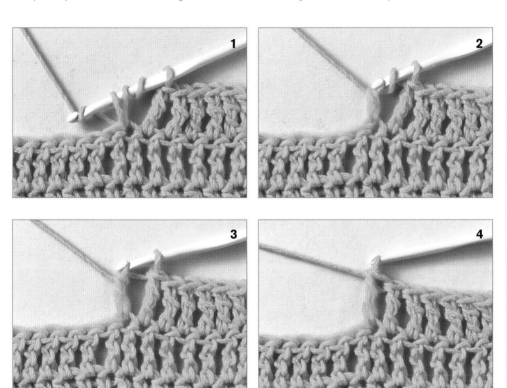

FRONT POST DOUBLE CROCHET

This stitch follows a row of double crochet. Chain 3 to turn. Wrap the yarn over the hook. Working from the front, insert the hook from right to left (left to right for left-handed crocheters) under the post of the first double crochet from the previous row, and pick up a loop (28). Wrap the yarn over the hook and complete the stitch as a double crochet.

Left-handed.

Right-handed.

BACK POST DOUBLE CROCHET

This stitch follows a row of double crochet. Chain 3 to turn. Wrap the yarn over the hook. Working from the back, insert the hook from right to left (left to right for left-handed crocheters) under the post of the first double crochet from the previous row, and pick up a loop (shown). Wrap the yarn over the hook and complete the stitch as a double crochet.

Left-handed.

Right-handed.

FRONT POST TRIPLE CROCHET

Follow the directions for Front Post Double Crochet (above), but begin by wrapping the yarn over the hook twice and complete the stitch as a triple crochet.

BOBBLE STITCH

Wrap the yarn over the hook and pick up a loop in the next stitch. Wrap the yarn over the hook again and pull it through 2 of the stitches on the hook. Repeat this 5 times in the same stitch. Then wrap the yarn over the hook and pull it through all 6 loops on the hook. The bobble stitch is worked from the wrong side and pushed to right side of the work.

CROSS STITCH

Skip 1 stitch, double crochet in the next stitch. Then double crochet in the skipped stitch by crossing the yarn in front of the stitch just made.

BLOCK STITCH

This stitch is worked after a row of double crochet stitches. Wrap the yarn over the hook and pick up a long loop in the next double crochet stitch from the previous row 4 times **(1)**. Pick up a loop in the next stitch and pull it through all ten loops on the hook **(2)**. Pick up a loop in the next stitch, chain 2 in that loop, and wrap the yarn over and through the 2 loops on the hook **(3)**.

BASIC TUNISIAN STITCH

Each row has 2 halves: picking up the loops and working them off.

Make a chain of the desired length.

Row 1 (first half): Keeping all loops on the hook, skip the first chain from the hook (the loop on the hook is the first chain) and draw up a loop in each chain across **(1)**. Do not turn.

Row 1 (second half): Wrap the yarn over the hook and draw it through the first loop. * Wrap the yarn over the hook and draw it through the next 2 loops. Repeat from * across until 1 loop remains. The loop that remains on the hook always counts as the first stitch of the next row **(2)**.

Row 2 (first half): Keeping all loops on the hook, skip the first vertical bar and draw up a loop under the next vertical bar and under each vertical bar across **(3)**.

Row 2 (second half): Work the same as the second half of row 1.

Repeat row 2 for basic Tunisian stitch.

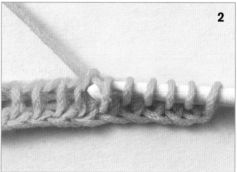

TUNISIAN AND SHELLS

Chain the number of stitches directed in the pattern.

Row 1 (foundation half shells, wrong side): Work 4 double crochets in the fourth chain from the hook (makes a half shell at the beginning of the row), * skip 3 chains, work 1 single crochet in next chain, skip 3 chains, and work 9 double crochets in next chain (makes a full shell). Repeat from * until 8 chains remain. Skip 3 chains, work 1 single crochet in the next chain, skip 3 chains, and work 5 double crochets in last chain (makes a half shell at the end of the row). Chain 1 and turn **(1)**.

Row 2 (Tunisian stitch, right side): * [Draw up a loop in the next stitch and retain the loop on the hook] 5 times (6 loops on the hook), draw up a loop in the next stitch and draw this loop through the first loop on the hook, forming an upright stitch or bar. [Yarn over and through 2 loops] 5 times *. There will be 6 bars in the row, and 1 loop left on the hook. The loop on the hook and the bar below it count as the first stitch. ** Retaining the loops on the hook, draw up a loop in each of the next 5 bars (6 loops on the hook), draw up a loop in the next stitch, and draw this loop through the first loop on the hook. [Yarn over and through 2 loops] 5 times. Repeat from ** 2 times. There will be 4 rows of bars **(2)**. Insert the hook in the second bar, yarn over and through the bar and the loop on the hook (1 stitch bound off), bind off 4 more stitches, and work 1 single crochet in the next stitch. Repeat from *, ending with a single crochet in the top of the turning chain. Chain 1 and turn. You now have blocks of Tunisian crochet between shells **(3)**.

Row 3: Skip the first stitch (chain 1 counts as the first stitch), work 1 single crochet in each stitch across the row, and work 1 single crochet in the turning chain. Chain 3 and turn **(4)**.

Row 4 (first half of full shells): Yarn over, draw up a loop in the second single crochet, yarn over and through 2 loops on the hook, [yarn over and draw up a loop in the next stitch, yarn over and through 2 loops] 3 times, yarn over and through 5 loops on the hook, and chain 1 tightly for the eye of the half shell **(5)**. * Chain 3, single crochet in the next stitch, chain 3, [yarn over and draw up a loop in the next stitch, yarn over and through 2 loops] 9 times, yarn over and through 10 loops on the hook, and chain 1 tightly to form the eye of the full shell. Repeat from * until all full shells are made. Chain 3, single crochet in the next stitch, chain 3, [yarn over and draw up a loop in the next stitch, yarn over and through 2 loops] 4 times, yarn over and through 5 loops, and chain 1 tightly to form the eye of the last half shell. Ch 3 and turn. You now have full shells between the Tunisian blocks **(6)**.

Row 5: Work 4 double crochets in the eye of the first half shell, skip chain 3, work 1 single crochet in the first single crochet, skip chain 3, * work 9 double crochets in the eye of the next shell, skip chain 3, work 1 single crochet in the next single crochet, and skip chain 3. Repeat from * until all the full shells are complete **(7)**. Skip chain 3, work 4 double crochets in the eye of last half shell, chain 1, and turn.

Repeat rows 2 through 5 for pattern.

PICKING UP STITCHES FOR BORDERS

Picking up stitches along the sides of a project, the row ends, is the hardest part of giving your crochet pieces a lovely finished look. It is worth the effort to practice a little to get this step just right.

The general rule of thumb is to pick up 1 stitch in every other row for single crochet **(1)**. For instance, if you have worked 20 rows of single crochet, you will pick up 10 stitches along the row ends. Pick up 1 stitch for every row for double crochet **(2)**. For instance, if you have worked 20 rows of double crochet, you will pick up 20 stitches. When picking up stitches on the edge of a Tunisian piece, pick up 1 stitch in each vertical bar along edge **(3)**. These guidelines work for most people, but not all. Your work must lie flat, and sometimes you will have to experiment to judge how to proceed. If your edges are rippling, like a ruffle, you are picking up too many stitches; if they are pulling in, you are picking up too few stitches. The best way to get an even edge is to divide the length to be worked into 4 parts. When the first section is done and lies flat, repeat that number of stitches for each of the following 3 sections. Work in every stitch of the top and bottom edges. Always work 3 stitches in each corner to make the project lie flat.

Abbreviations

approx	approximately		**p**	picot
beg	begin/beginning		**patt**	pattern
bet	between		**pc**	popcorn
BL	back loop(s)		**pm**	place marker
BP	back post		**prev**	previous
BPdc	back post double crochet		**rem**	remain/remaining
CC	contrasting color		**rep**	repeat(s)
ch	chain		**rev sc**	reverse single crochet
ch-	refers to chain or space previously made, e.g., ch-1 space		**rnd(s)**	round(s)
			RS	right side(s)
ch lp	chain loop		**sc**	single crochet
ch-sp	chain space		**sc3tog**	single crochet 3 stitches together
CL	cluster(s)		**sk**	skip
cm	centimeter(s)		**Sl st**	slip stitch
cont	continue		**sp(s)**	space(s)
dc	double crochet		**st(s)**	stitch(es)
dc2tog	double crochet 2 stitches together		**tbl**	through back loop
dec	decrease/decreases/decreasing		**tch**	turning chain
dtr	double triple crochet		**tog**	together
FL	front loop(s)		**tr**	triple crochet
foll	follow/follows/following		**WS**	wrong side(s)
FP	front post		**yd**	yard(s)
FPdc	front post double crochet		**yo**	yarn over
FPtr	front post triple crochet		**yoh**	yarn over hook
g	gram(s)		**[ ]**	Work instructions within brackets as many times as directed
hdc	half double crochet		**( )**	At end of row, indicates total number of stitches worked
inc	increase/increases/increasing			
lp(s)	loop(s)		*****	Repeat instructions following the single asterisk as directed
m	meter(s)		******	Repeat instructions between asterisks as many times as directed or repeat from a given set of instructions
MC	main color			
mm	millimeter(s)			
oz	ounce(s)			